LIFT OFF!

TRAINS

Joy Richardson

WATTS BOOKS
London • New York • Sydney

On track

Even before there were trains, rail tracks were used to help heavy wagons run smoothly. People or horses did the pulling.

Today there are millions of miles of railway track criss-crossing every country in the world.

Trains carry people and goods along the tracks to their destination.

Steam trains

The first trains were pulled along by steam engines.

Steam engines work by burning coal to heat water in the boiler. This makes steam which drives rods connected to the wheels.

Behind the engine there is a tender which carries the coal supplies.

Steam engines can pull lots of heavy wagons or carriages for passengers.

Fuel supply

For one hundred years, almost
all trains ran on steam.
Now most trains use
diesel or electric power.

Diesel trains burn diesel
fuel which comes from oil.

Electric trains use electricity
from conductor rails on the track
or from an overhead cable.

An arm on top of the train
keeps in touch with the cable
as the train speeds along.

On the rails

Underneath each part of the train
there are wheels attached
to a metal framework.
The wheels fit on to the rail
and grip the inside edge.

The rails are fixed to
cross bars called sleepers.

The distance between the
rails must be exactly the
same all along the track.
Most trains run on rails
about a metre and a half apart.

Wheel

Rail

Sleeper

Signal work

On busy lines, lots of trains
use the same stretch of track.
Signals keep the trains apart.

A red light means stop.
A green light means go.

Where the track divides,
points move the rails to keep
the train on the right track.

Displays in the signalbox show
where each train has got to.

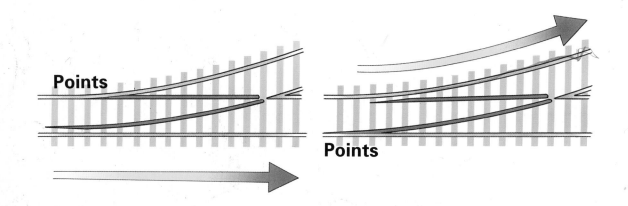

Points

Points

Stopping the train

The driver watches the
line ahead from the cab.
There are controls for starting
and stopping the train
and for changing speed.

There are brakes on wheels
under every coach or wagon.
When the driver puts on the brakes,
all the wheels slow down.

In an emergency, passengers
can pull a handle to stop the train.

Carrying heavy loads

Trains carry passengers and take letters and parcels across the country.

Freight trains carry heavy loads from place to place.

Different kinds of wagons can be linked up to carry coal, oil tanks, tree trunks, or huge containers from place to place.

All this freight must be organised so that it can be collected easily at the other end.

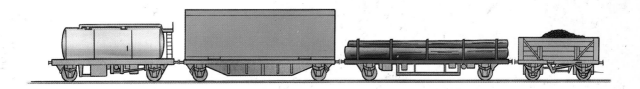

Climbing high

Trains find climbing difficult.

The early railway engineers
built tunnels through hills and
viaducts over valleys to
keep the trains on a level track.

Tracks wind slowly round hillsides.
If the climb is too steep,
the train wheels will slip.

Special mountain railways
have a cog wheel which grips a
toothed rail in the middle of the track.

Under the ground

Underground trains carry
people across busy cities.

They travel through tunnels
deep under the streets.

The trains run on electricity
from a conductor rail on the track.

Electronic systems control the
signals and make trains stop.
The doors open automatically.

Some underground trains could
operate without a driver.

High-speed trains

New high-speed trains can
carry people from city to city
almost as fast as an aeroplane.

Electricity comes from overhead cables.
There are electric motors under
each carriage to help drive the wheels.

The fastest trains run on special
straight tracks with no signals.

High-speed trains are
streamlined like aeroplanes.
This helps to stop the rush of
air from slowing them down.

Changing trains

Light railways are being built
to carry passengers speedily
over short distances.

Monorail trains run along
or hang from a single rail.
They can carry people
high above the ground.

Maglevs are a new type
of train without rails.
Magnets lift the train and make
it glide along above the track.

Trains are changing fast.

Train facts

The fastest train is the French high-speed train which reached speeds of over 500 km per hour.

The fastest thing on rails was a rocket powered sledge which reached almost 10,000 km per hour. There was no-one in it.

There are narrow gauge railways in Britain with rails as little as 26 cm apart.

Index

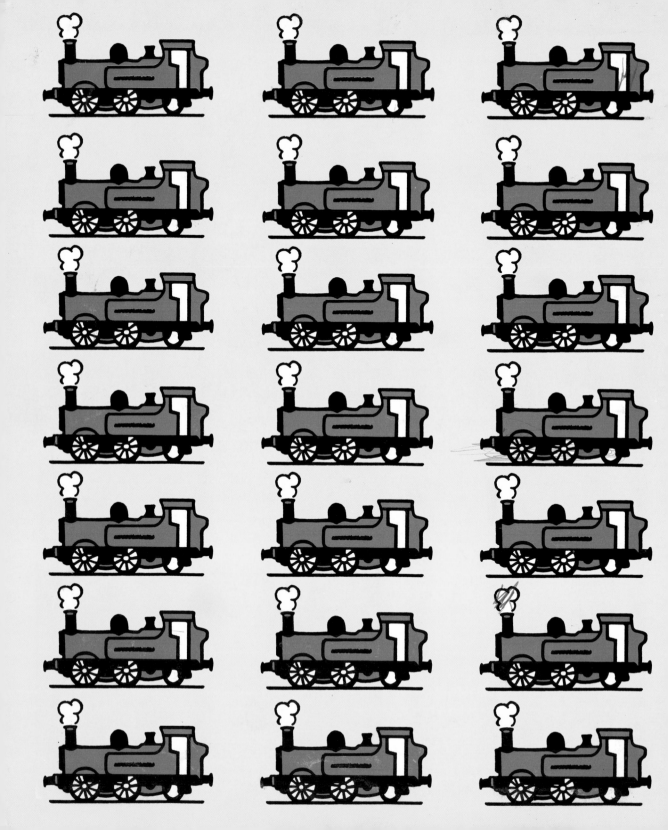